next to last words

Also by Daniel Hoffman

POETRY

The Whole Nine Yards: Longer Poems
Makes You Stop and Think: Sonnets
Beyond Silence: Selected Shorter Poems, 1948–2003
Darkening Water
Middens of the Tribe
Hang-Gliding from Helicon
Brotherly Love
The Center of Attention
Striking the Stones
Broken Laws
The City of Satisfactions
A Little Geste
An Armada of Thirty Whales

PROSE

Zone of the Interior: A Memoir, 1942–1947
Words to Create a World
Faulkner's Country Matters
Barbarous Knowledge: Myth in the Poetry of Yeats, Graves, and Muir
Poe Poe Poe Poe Poe Poe Poe
Form and Fable in American Fiction
The Poetry of Stephen Crane
Paul Bunyan, Last of the Frontier Demigods

TRANSLATION

A Play of Mirrors, poems by Ruth Domino

AS EDITOR

Over the Summer Water, poems by Elizabeth McFarland
Ezra Pound and William Carlos Williams
Harvard Guide to Contemporary American Writing
American Poetry and Poetics
The Red Badge of Courage and Other Tales

next to last words

poems

by
Daniel Hoffman

LOUISIANA STATE UNIVERSITY PRESS
BATON ROUGE

Published by Louisiana State University Press
Copyright © 2013 by Daniel Hoffman
All rights reserved
Manufactured in the United States of America

Designer: Michelle A. Neustrom
Typeface: Bembo

Library of Congress Cataloging-in-Publication Data

Hoffman, Daniel, 1923–
   Next to last words : poems / Daniel Hoffman.
   p. cm.
   "LSU Press Paperback Original."
   Includes bibliographical references.
   ISBN 978-0-8071-5022-1 (pbk. : alk. paper) — ISBN 978-0-8071-5023-8 (pdf) — ISBN 978-0-8071-5024-5 (epub) — ISBN 978-0-8071-5025-2 (mobi)
   I. Title.
   PS3515.O2416N49 2013
   811'.54—dc23

2012020863

The paper in this book meets the guidelines for permanence and durability of the Committee on Production Guidelines for Book Longevity of the Council on Library Resources. ∞

i.m.

Elizabeth McFarland Hoffman

Contents

I

To Undisclosed Recipient— *3*
At 89 *4*
The Day *6*
A Riddle *7*
Why They Are Not All Alike *8*
Disturbers of the Peace *9*
True North *10*
Other Bodies *11*
Interplanetary Converse *12*
First Coyote *13*
Awareness *15*
Raven *17*

II

Freneau *21*
A Democratic Vista *24*
1931 *26*
A Casualty, 1946 *27*
Rage *29*
In Memory of Lewis Corey *31*
Mishap off Seal Rock *34*
Ninth Street, 1952 *36*
Siren Song *37*
Reading the News, 1968 *38*
Autumn *40*
History, 1989 *41*

III

The Hill *45*
At the Winter Solstice *47*
A Household Tale *48*
Icons *49*
Life-Lines *51*
Spring *53*
Darts, 1965 *54*

IV

Eve Reclining *59*
For Whom I Make This Song *60*
Then *61*
A Poe Taster *62*
A Happy Poet *63*
Last Words *65*
Bands *66*
The Key *68*
Night Journey *71*
Today *73*
Soul *74*
Afterlife *75*

Acknowledgments 77
Notes 79
About the Author 83

I

To Undisclosed Recipient—

Yes, you! *You're* the Lucky One. No, not
because your e-mail address won the draw
of a lottery you hadn't entered—£1,250,000—
nor are you the designated beneficiary

of a Nigerian millionaire whose widow can't
get his money out of the country unless
you accept a 20% commission—
nor need you fill in your age, or gender, or

your bank account, or send $3,000 deposit now—
No, no, your luck is none of these, but if you will
just turn these pages, and read what's in this book—
That's where you'll find your luck. Good luck!

At 89

Still two years older,
My stillborn brother
Whose murmured advice is
My solace in crises
Has passed ninety now.
So I asked him, How
Will I find it ahead
Through my tenth decade?

Surely he heard . . .

He must have heard . . .

No reply, not a word,
So I knew that I
Was being told
—No reply's a reply—
What my future would hold . . .

But I will refuse
His null prophecy
And despite aging's pains,
Till from this life sundered
At over a hundred,
With the strength that remains,
I, while I can, choose
The alternative—
It subsists and sustains
What will befall
All that ensues,

As in daily routines
With the intensest
Bequests of the senses,
And will not let perish
The memories I cherish
None else can recall;

Among joys it may give,
Even loss unconsoled
Keeps heart growing old
While I'll live, while I'll live,
I'll live, live, live.

The Day
(for Robert Penn Warren)

The sun has rent
that bolt of mourning-cloth
unfolded on the stars, the trees, the houses.
Now the mites and swirls of lint
dance between the hemlocks and the maples.
Everything's alive. We stir,
We step out on the porch, we breathe

this light that sifts
through vanished moontrack, over the leaves.
History is happening
beyond this hill.
Clouds, impersonal
as institutions, work their will,
improve the fallow fields of heaven

while afar, the syllables
that will comprise
this evening's headlines mutter
as though the skies would shudder
reverberant
at their surmise
as we watch the children

back from school, from soccer,
go forth in pairs, to the movies and return
gaily having made their way
a little toward a destination
of which the day
only this morning was a part.

A Riddle

I am the chink between two voids.
I clasp both links of an endless chain.
Who knows me knows there is no repose.
I come once, then never again.
I burst the webs of all men's cunning.
None can hold me and none detain me.
None can preserve me, none restrain me.
I am end, I am beginning—

[This moment]

Why They Are Not All Alike

In Mexico she'd found a carpenter
Who so pleased her with his painted chair

She, on impulse, asked that he make three more,
Identical, a charming set of four.

She came to pick them up. She hadn't dickered
To reduce the price, but now surmised

She might get four for only thrice the sticker
For the first one. But how then surprised

She was to learn, for four, that the expense
Was as for *five!* Now, how did that make sense?

He replied he'd have to charge her more
—Repeating what he's made would be a bore,

And, as for creating new designs, prevents
His carving painted chairs not seen before.

Disturbers of the Peace

Well, where would *they* be
Without peace?
As for those with broken-

Rhythmed poems, how wring
Subtleties
From jabs of tongue and stutter

Against remembered hymn or hum?
But
Reality, in our time, demands . . . All

Right, then, let a mirror's
Cracks compose in jagged
Reflected glints the real

Spectrum
From our refractory illusion,
The singleness of light.

True North

It's only an idea, an approximation
Of the Back of the North Wind
Where we've never been,

A place none but the spirits
Who howl in storms have seen.
Not even the pole of the earth

Can point it out.
In the cold, cold sky
Wavering

From the star we call North
Toward another
As yet unnamed.

Other Bodies

In their grand
imperturbability the planets
must have their own

fish to fry. Why should they
worry at what they shine on
down here, though we

send up satellites in manned
and unmanned orbits prying
into their business—

we let those other bodies find
their own solutions
to problems

of astronomical proportions
the way they give
carte blanche to us

to cope with ours.

Interplanetary Converse

(i.m. Baruch Blumberg)

Now that we know the Milky Way is made
Of stars in billions larger than the sun,
Many ringed by planets of their own
With oceans, canals, and ponds in centigrade
Temperatures that could let life emerge,
Eager for converse, we've digitized our queries
In English, the universal language, curious
If other planets' creatures have converged
Like ours.
Well, how can we be but annoyed,
As through 300 light years we've tried to reach,
Inviting their response, yet from the void
We're graced by neither intercourse nor speech
Between us, orbiting our puny Phoebus,
And out in space, bacilli or amoebas.

First Coyote

Last night the sky paled
where the full round eye of the moon
poured its gaze down

watching spruces at the edge
of the berryfield rustle
and their long shadows reach

out on the field watching
the creature skulking
between the granite schists

among the silent berrybushes
and the moon's eye poured
its pallor down amid the crying-out

of a wild desire that tore the silence,
tore the cool night air between the boulders,
tore our sleep behind the blinds.

I shone the torch against the hillside,
its hose of light splashed on hillocks
until, between the boulders, two

emerald gleams returned my beam,
then the creature turned him sideways
to leap into a hidden gulley

with its dog's head and high haunches
and the lean back sloping down,
tail's brush held out behind

—Never seen so big a fox or
heard a fox make such a howl
by the full moon till now

though many a moonlit or dark night
foxes climb the granite shafts
and stab the dark, or the light, with sharp

barks that echo ... not like this
howl of a captive tied
to a burning stake beneath the moon.

Awareness

That unwritten poem is burdening your mind,
How get it started while the world around you
Is filled with importunate distractions? The poem's
A swollen cloud that won't set free its rain.
So strip your senses naked—then they can
Sniff and see, can taste, can touch
Your poem, can listen as it moves,
Then concentrate upon that poem you'd write,
Look inward, inward, withhold attention
From the ceaseless energy of the sun which feeds
The bright, then brighter minutes of the morning
To burn its path into the center of the day,
You must ignore the wind arriving from
A place horizons hide, tousling the meadow,
Leaving unannounced for some distant, still
Sierra where it may bring rains, rains
Hooding the sky with rumpled clouds amid
The line-storm's slashes, jets of ozone flashing
Among the trees, the clearing after, glisten
On each leaf and stem of Queen Anne's Lace
Nodding in its dewy mantle, fretwork
Of the stems supporting blossoms
In a woven elegance of white,
The burnished Indian Paintbrush, vivid, hairy
Leaves still clutching beads of rain,
The mica on the rocks beneath now glinting,
Holding the secret silence of the snake
Coiling and unplaiting coils across
Its crevices, unheard by you or by
The field mouse nibbling as you withdraw
Attention from the clouds convening over
The distant hill, nor mind annunciations

They prepare for the tournament of colors
Of the evening when the caucus of
The white throat's whistle, redwing's juicy chirr,
The jay's rude scoffs and the deceptive
Repertoire of one ventriloquial catbird
Hush, all hushed but for the distant pealing
Of reclusive woodthrush in the swale,
To none of which you listen, giving all
Awareness to your still unwritten poem.

Raven

I was there where nothing was before the world was made.
I saw the work before the First Day's end,
Perched on the Maker's collarbone while he tried to amend
His first error.

I swayed on the rooftree above the coupled beasts,
Was first to break out of the wooden womb of the ark,
On all that surging water the only spot of dark
Was my shadow.

Oh but I was a songster in the days before the flood!
Till I found on Ararat the tables of the law
And sang the future when I had cracked the code—
Cronk! Cronk!

II

Freneau

No one had heard the honeysuckle
raise its trumpets for aboriginal
annunciations—
           A seed
bursts, and now the hillside's giddy
with this wild perfume that clings
to, then on inshore breezes, spreads
across the land.
           Of shades
gliding in ghost canoes
toward embers glowing in the long
house of memory—
           These
like Roman senators in loincloths
persist, ennobled by stoic sufferings,
under colonnades of trees.
Who else would purify them
of their savagery and set
their images upon
our plinths?
           The very year
he whittled verses from the native wood
his country
           Kicked free, taking
the name "Republic," and bequeathing
to every mother's son the cares
of State, since all men are good
enough to govern here.

           All men defend us
from cabals of office seekers,
office holders, tongues like knives drawn

for tavern brawls and liars
in public places poisoning the well
of truth.

                Ripe for improvement,
the land is gouged. Summer
darkens with the stench of burning
flesh. How write of ghosts
or bumblebees and blossoms in
this foetid air?

                Strolling
down Broadway, he feels the fit
come on him, seized
by the least engaging of them all,
her stern brow demanding angry style.
Who drives sweet Fancy into exile
but that splenetic songstress, Satire?
In this free land he thinks of Dryden, Pope—
not to be savored here, their liberty
within the rules of art . . .

            In haste
to sound the trump of an opinion
—policy his spur—he pulls a pinion
from his wing to pen for partisan neighbors
each sputtering column whose couplets clash
like sabers. Avid
that the Future mind his name,
how could he,
first poet of the Republic, know

which verse of his
the centuries would winnow,
or that, recalling him, would nail his fame
to Washington's retort,

        "That rascal, Freneau."

A Democratic Vista

The poets were speaking at the Symposium
On Poetry and the National Purpose, attended
By many in the crowd, many poets and lovers
Of poetry and many lovers of poets
While one of the poets, the one I'll call
The Poet, was telling the crowd, especially
The members thereof who themselves were in fact
Not poets, that nothing is as significant as Poets,
For it is poets who are the prophets of the race,
As well as its annalists, yes, its analysts who notice not
Only what has happened and is happening to the race
But announce beforehand what is going to happen
—And that isn't all, they make it happen,
They change your lives—while, as I say, The Poet
Was saying all this and the crowded crowd
Was brought to the verge of cheers while
He was chanting the terrific openness of the ego
Like a continent uncontained by the roiling steel
Breakers of any sea, he celebrates the openness
Of the great variety counter as plentitudinous as appetites,
Making of everything the ingredients for a possible
Though unexampled ingestion whether of delight
Disgust or what for others would be terror
Like the knowledge of his own death
Which becomes only one layer in his hero sandwich
Surrounded with relish by the cries of the suffering
The outcasts the whores the battle-losers
And captains of wrecked ships all
Equally in the feast and of the feast and
At the feast with the color green the shouts
Of victory and the amorous bodies
Of young men—you might not think so but it proved

That this unmetered and immeasurable readiness
To keep from being fenced in by anything by being
The self that does the including, excluding
Nothing but tragedy—this, this is the American
Way. The Camerado for whom he waits
At the end of the long road, *c'est nous,*
The children spawned in the open nets
Of his liberties. Between his long spiels
It's we who pick up our tickets at the Thruway
Tollbooths, erect new shopping centers in the interstices
Of his strophes to the Future, growing older
While his leaves rattle in the wind. We turn
The page to see his Democratic Vista—"Never
Was there more hollowness of heart . . . the underlying
Principles of the States are not honestly believed in
Nor is the human itself believed in," he told us before
A century and a half had brought us to the future
He believed in, saying, "I know nothing grander,
More positive proof of the past, the triumphant
Result of faith in human-kind than a well-contested
American national election," a sentiment
Perhaps we'd better leave Open-
                                      ended—

1931

Bounty coinciding with desire,
Our shares aggrandized while the lawn was mown,
But now the baker's tray of eclairs oozes
In the warmth of windowed sun. Patched sleeves
Clutch stones and sticks the whole block long.
The rotogravure frames revolutions
In strange gabled towns, dimly historical.
Above the roof at noon, in lunch-hour hush,
The President of our First National Trust, thoughtful,
High in the open window, noon, spread-eagle-armed,
Plunges toward the Post Road's asphalt fascination
—The sudden crowd swirls like confetti moving
Under a teacup sky afloat with bonbons
Toward him, then in a wild rush toward the door
As paint peels from pillars and men fight
Over coal chunks dropped from trains. In the rank steam
Of alleys of thin soup where frayed investors
Cough and the light wanes, they warm their soles
At fires in rusted cans while Thorstein
And dour Thomas, Frederick and Karl hold
Meetings elsewhere, pass a resolution
Censuring simple Adam for his base trust in
All he trusted while we dreamed.

A Casualty, 1946

His life is a hangover after a party he can hardly remember.
His days as blank as the pages
On a pad of unfilled prescriptions,
Rx to relieve this patient's sense
Of the pain of being
Of so little consequence.
Write down here on the pad
What he must do
To become a source
Of concern in others.

He must do something.

He has something he must do.
He is remembering the party after which his days
Became as tedious as a hangover without a cure.
He remembers
The whistle of bombs screaming down from the sky
On another city
Far away, he remembers
The pang that squeezed his breath
When the sirens howled
And he was on furlough in the tube riding toward her
But not yet with her
Or in the pub waiting for her to come to meet him,

It was with the pain that something
Might happen to someone
Other than himself,
Which he has not felt since
It did.

And she whose ways with a man he still remembers
Through the long hangover of the red-rimmed years,
The touch of her fingers clasping his head
The parting of her lips her thighs her body
Awakening to frenzy
He can still remember.

He must set it down
On the blank page
So he'll never forget—

His head dulled his eyes adrift in
The bleary gaze of the nonconvivial drinker
He struggles to use stale words
And their tired conventions,

He feels the reeling energy again
That blazed from their encounter
To etch the dull green walls, the carved arm of the chair,
The cut-glass ashtray and the antimacassar
Into his memory as he remembers them

But the words
On his page evoke
Nothing.

It takes more than suffering
And trials to write well,
To live without love
And be unable to tell
What one has lost is
A special kind of hell.

Rage

Coming out of his brain is a common fuse.
It leads to the tinder
box in his gut.

How much of a spark does it take to catch
on the braided thread
of his self-concern

and set it to sputter and sputter and fume?
Once lit, it's not likely
to go out, but burn

shorter and closer. It's only a matter
of time till the fire
pries inward and out

of himself he is hurled by the force of his rage—
nothing of him
is contained in his skin.

From his chest bursts a blast in a curse
of fists and lips
uncover weapons.

He spins in a cloud where there is no center.
His mind is struck blind
by the black jets that pound

in spurts through his arteries. Wrath spews forth
like an oil-well seething
afire in his heart.

The hurt he's become is all he can feel.
His world's a wound
that will not heal.

In Memory of Lewis Corey

[born Luigi Fraina]

I
(1944–1953)

He knew I'd never be a true disciple
When I coughed, embarrassed by his love
For Swinburne. Then, I thought,
A real reformer ought
To praise revolt in *everything.*
But he'd no use for verse that didn't 'sing.'
And so he taught
(I didn't know it for a lesson yet)
That poetry and politics don't mix
In simple rhetorics. You can see
How young I was, how out of fashion he.
I since have read of Fraina in a book,
How Madison Square Garden rose and shook
At his command, one of ten thousand voices
Vowing to free
From imperialist invasion
Archangel far across the sea.
But what's all that to me?
I wasn't even born when Fraina led
His fractious splinter in those Red
Matchstick plays at power.
The man I honor is the man I knew—
Self-purged before the Moscow Trials,
He came through
The withering away, as at the stake,
Of every vow his fervent youth could make
But one, and that the most romantic trust

That, shown the injustice of our institutions,
We will choose to make them just.

Corey had long done with revolutions,
But I confess, I haven't found mankind
As sensible as he to what enlightened mind
Describes as the common good
To a self-seeking multitude.
It's fifteen years he dead now, yet the thought
Of Corey makes my mind rehearse
All that he taught,
And this thought chides—
How little else have I reformed besides
The diction of my verse.
Should the commonwealth, like art, seek perfect forms,
What can it learn from my self-searching trade?
Those were the images he made,
Those, and the image of a man possessed
By reason to persuade
A race spoon-fed upon self-interest
To set the table, break its hoarded bread.
What can I do with his bequest
Who wished no man to suffer wrong,
But make his memory a song?

II
(1953–1968)

It was a time that cowardice
Begat upon disgrace;
What else had numbed all decent sense
In so many in high place,

While those whom popular hatred fed
Rose up by being base,
>   *—As we may remember.*

They tarred him with black printer's ink,
They smeared him in the town,
They bought a hireling liar
To cry his good name down.
But what can harm his spirit now?
He's gone to his renown.
>   *—As we may remember.*

For he's an honored citizen
In the republic of the dead,
And we who were his countrymen
—Now let the truth be said—
May learn to cut our plenty's loaf
With his blessing on our bread.
>   *—With his blessing on our bread.*

Mishap off Seal Rock

When they saw the early sun
leap crazily about,
glinting from the sway
of the capsized gun-
metal off Seal Rock,

Seth Haskell and his crew,
Joey, Dave, and Paul,
together had to haul
the out-of-stater
over the gunnels.

—in these waters only
a damned fool would fool
with such a cockleshell,
his wrist swelled in a knot
of the line to the lobsterpot—

his arm wrapped
not at the float end,
They had to cut the line
to free the trap.
Wedged beneath the seat

in his tippy craft
they found a fifth three-
quarters gone—booze
he didn't need
For—cold sober, he'd

pull another's pot.
It sure looks like there's
someone, somewhere,
sees what he deserved,
he got.

Ninth Street, 1952

The air peels from the scorching walls.
Noon. July. Half a mile away
Broken echoes of the brass band stir
Limp strips of sound on a catspaw breeze.
At Independence Hall faint ceremonies
But Ninth Street's cobbles bake like swelling loaves
Not stirring even when the scream repeats
Its scream, the scream nearing the hospital,
A scream that staggers through the side-door
Beneath the cupola and as the woman sways
On high heels lurching in electric-blue
Dress the scream still screams through her black hand
Held against her face to stop the scream
That screams its jets of blood from a slashed eye
And dribbles on dry stones beside the dry
Trough the S.P.C.A. gave the neighborhood—
'A Merciful Man is Merciful to His Beast' can barely
Be traced in the grime where thirsty horses stood.

Siren Song

After weeks of fog, the stillness
of this first day—at last
the silent blue sky spreading
above the whistle of the white-throat
and, in the cove, the crazy laughter
of, between dives, a single loon

when the air is shattered by the shrill
red screams, disaster's aria
as an ambulance cuts across the beach
and up past the house, then swerves
in the turn to some cottage we cannot see,
where a neighbor may be dying

while, as the siren fades
in the woods, the day
goes on unperturbed, the sparrows
continuing their tweedles
to one another as though nothing,
nothing, nothing has occurred.

Reading the News, 1968

We wake to find
The world's folded
Disasters

At our door
The deadlines tell
Declines and falls

The ineradicable poor
Fester in the sump
Of our city where

Foetid wastes between
Condemned walls
Seethe all year

A redcar siren
Flails between the bars
A curse

Like white iron
Tells who should turn
The other cheek

Who burn
Where the mild and meek
Inherit nothing

Where rage begets
Nothing
The night sweats

As in a dream
Unmelting fear
Spells on a graven gate

Who Enter Here
Abandon . . . What
vengeful diatribe

Or redemptory
Plan will this
Day inscribe?

Autumn

The summer people have taken
Their SUVs down numbered highways
Leaving the sea to clutch

At shorefront footage
And their boarded cottages
While inland, on back roads

Past the pulped-out woodlots, winter
People in their unpainted houses
On the untilled farms

Stare through window-frames
At yards surrounded
By broken kiddie-cars, old tires, clam creels,

Or divine the promise of their future
From frayed configurations in the entrails
Of aged automobiles.

History, 1989

(June 5th)

Yes, you've seen him, skinny guy
in a white tee-shirt on the road,
arms outstretched, stopping traffic
as though to let a mother safely cross
with children, while the smoking

tank at the column's head in idle
roars, another dozen stretched
behind in a dragon's tail,
cannons pointing past him toward
the square, the statue, students singing,

the whole formation's order thwarted
by one youth standing in the way,
so now, on clanking caterpillar
treads, the head tank executed
a ponderous manoeuver, turning

to the right as though to pass him
but he, nimble-footed, skips
a couple of sideways steps and stands
arms outstretched before the cannon
as before . . . there now ensues

a curious *pas de deux:* the huge
squat tank lurching sideways
as though to pass him, but he again
nimbly skips, leftward now,
and it faces him, arrested still

—we've seen this, but we couldn't see
what my former student, teaching
English, with her pupils there
saw when the cameras turned away—
a dozen soldiers rushed him,

roughed him down an alley. One
shot to the head. The tanks lurch
forward eager to do their brutal
work, as unhindered power continues
its practices, while history,
learning nothing from itself,

inscribes another page in red.
Terror and death. What lingers, though,
is the courage, facing death,
of one man to oppose its swath,
one man, standing in the way.

III

The Hill

The hill beside this farm is one of those places on earth
for which no myth has ever been made.
True, the islands

out in the bay were the head, the hoofs, the haunches
of the Great Moose that was slain by Glu'uskap
who in Penobscot

times came back from the underground river and broke
Old Windbird's wing to tame the winds,
but no one says

his name, not even the Indian blueberry rakers
over the road—they're down from Old Town,
a different tribe.

This hill was never the breast of the earth goddess;
no one has seen the souls of the dead
come out of its womb

and dance on the peak in a ring on All Souls' Night
when the devil was fiddler, no ancient folk
dwell in its bowels:

This is a craggy rockheap with a jagged crown
of Maine spruces and a boulder-strewn field
at the top. The gulls

swing on the updrafts over the hill and a stream
carries the runoff into the swale.
In alder thickets

at the base of the slope by day the deer are sleeping,
at night they roam on their silent trails
while the foxes

yelp from cairns of rude stones and the silence
of the ancient wilderness breaks again
as the hill returns

an echo. What can the centuries mean to a hill?
When the Penobscots slept on the beach beside
    their fires by the bay

and at dawn set off in canoes for the glistening islands
they took with them their tales. As for us, coming after,
we have no myths to tell.

At the Winter Solstice

Austerity is not asperity

as the woodchuck and the snoozing owl
in oak's high hollow or blackberry root
sheltering feathered claw and fallow foot
against the winter's rude temerity
know well.

Then prosper them within the earthy hostel—

let time of ice-caps and the soughing
hemlocks' sleet-sleeved pentecost
annunciate the coming of their host
in a risen guise of the green gospel
at the sun's sowing.

A Household Tale

Jack thought it luck, but all was foreordained,
To buy a cow, then trade the cow for beans.
Mother's saga was the bitter cup of one
Supported by a sweet but simple son.
At least he meant well,
She thinks, hobbling on her crutch,
Watering the stupid seeds as night fell
And so to bed. Jack in his garret sees
The moonstruck mighty stalk arising
From its slit between earth-mounds like knees
And *whoosh,* he's out the window, on the roof,
Now rising with the beans,
What else would be there, at the top, but
A huge castle where the bearded
Ogre with his thunderous brows
Seeks vengeance on the naughty boy
Who penetrated his wife's oven,
And he the monster married to a lovely
Supple lady who could not escape him,
For she hobbles since he broke her leg
And his one appetite's for shepherd pie
Baked of carrots, crust, and boy. But she
Will hide Jack in her broom closet
Till he can stick his dirk—he's brought a dirk—
Into the giant's belly
And repossess the castle and the lady,
For look, the truth is, all is Jack's
Left him by his dear old Dad.

Icons

No one now expects the rough
Hilarity of Cruikshank
—The flight of hands like larks
Beneath the high sprig of mistletoe
From lacy wrists surrounding
Pinchwaisted beauties'
Bosoms like Devon cream
Spilling out as they bend
Over the hairy boar's
Head's mouth in its idiot grin

Munching an apple—
All that is gone now
With such emblems as the green
Live tree, live holly
Greens, live children,
Cousins, aunts, clustered
Beneath real candles
At the knees of Mother
In shirtwaist and stays,
Papa in his Prince Albert—the
Extended family's a divided
Host now, we can hardly
Keep in touch by long

Distance calls; the season's
Cheer since orange moons
And black cats disappeared
The day past Hallowe'en
Is manifested to us by
Rudolph the Red-Nosed Rein-
Deer, the pink bulb twinkling

In his plastic nose,
And over the P.A. system's

Speakers beneath the blue
Aluminum glittering trees
On lampposts come the stories
Of not particularly hallowed
Refrains—reminders still,
In a forgetful time, of more
Archaic icons,
Boars' heads or the Yule
Log sizzling, a cradle
Ringed by dazed cows, a tired
Pale woman resting,
And on their knees

Rascals in silk pajamas,
Three Druids, or is it kings?
Not even Matthew tells
Their names, their home addresses,
Occupations, ID numbers,
Who, wiser than Herod, bring
Tribute in the spirit
Of the simple and the creatures
Acknowledging a mystery
Not their aristocracy
Nor the merchant wisdom
Of any of their empires
Can at any cost ignore.

Life-Lines

(for Richard Eberhart)

Morning,
and the mist hangs
close

upon the water.
Islands
disappear. Trees,

ledges, melt
into a sameness
of white light.

Awaking
to the world's
obliteration,

but for his ox
alone, alone
on Hog Island,

Fred Carver
would holler
'Halloo! . . . Halloo! . . . ?'

into the gleaming
still droplets,
hollered 'Halloo . . . ?'

Till slipping
through the silvered
selvedge of

the long lapping
silence, higher
pitched, from Mr. Beal

atop his unseen
tower on Pumpkin
Island Lighthouse

three miles down
the charted bay,
a faint *'Halloo! . . .'*

testified
the whole world's
still there

unchanged
since sundown
yesterday.

Spring

All the holes
in hollow trees
and crevices

beneath the eaves
are teeming now
with snouts

of small squirrels
and the imperative
craws of featherless

starlings ready
ready ready to devour
devour devour devour the world.

Darts, 1965

Summer spent exploring
In Yeats's noble canon
His heroes' *sprezzatura*,
But now, an overnight
Stay en route to Shannon

In Bally-something-or-other
With its castle that beguiles
The traveller to ignore
The grimy factory
Where men are making tiles—

Tiles and tourists, here
These are the only two
Ways to turn a shilling.
My brimming mug of beer
Is drawn by a colleen,

Mere child, maybe thirteen.
Her Dad is publican.
I'm the only tourist;
Hard at their game of darts
The workers, boy and man,

Play for sixpence a game.
They ask, Will I play with them?
I've been at darts all summer,
But for these lads—Darts
Is a way of life with them!

First, from eight and a half feet
You must hit the outer rim

Of the target, only half an inch wide
Before your score can count.
Was I drag on our side!

The others were well on their way
To a perfect 601
When my scoring had barely begun.
They played with confident grace
And concentration,

Keeping well out of mind
The dingy hovels they lived in,
Raw fires in the kilns of clay,
The long, long years of their bleak
Labor, their mingy pay.

Next morning I turn aside
From the movie on TWA,
I close my eyes, am with friends
At the dartboard again as we play
Keeping well out of mind

As they did, that they
Would be toiling at tiles again
While I'm flying home.
For their ale, for the fun of our game
They'd not let me pay.

IV

Eve Reclining

(Musée Rolin, Autun)

Beneath indulgent berries and forked leaves
In stone Eve indolently lies so lightly
She seems suspended in the buoyant air.
Her flesh, formed from a rib of Adam's dust,
Still incandescent from the breath of heaven—
What infinite possibilities of joy
Does her tranced gaze command?
Inscrutable, her face; her plaited hair
Coils upon a pliant arm. She brushes
Succulent fruit hung from the yielding branch.

There is no serpent anywhere.

For Whom I Make This Song

There is but one for whom I make this song.
For her the cockerel sun in honey steeps
His sheaves of light that rise like summer grain—
He'd sow the world with light, to gaze on her!
O when she turns the whole sky turns with her.
She seethes the malty marrow of my blood—
I, just to watch her, feel my rooted soul
Wheel, a green tall dizzying Maypole.

O what a gallantry of grace attends
The slightest dancing of her wrists and knees—
I had not thought that Nature or my kind
Could bear within our frangible human form
Such annunciation. Where she comes
Combs of honey burst on my five wits.
I can relive it all, all hallowing:
Merely to think upon her is to sing.

[1957]

Then

A familiar room with sunlight leaping
Between the shutters to the bed,
The gleam of beams importunate on your head,
Your fine hair bronzed and silvered and your white
Throat lain back, lips a little open,
The wordless silence broken, broken
By the moan of that delight
By which the world was made.
When the blaze our bodies kindled
Flared in joy, then dwindled
Till the flame no longer played
As we sank like falling stars . . .

Lying alone, in single
Reverie, I'd pierce the dark
With memory, as though recalled
Exultation could make the embers
Of now unappeasable desire,
Thinking of you, as then,
Bring back that fire.

A Poe Taster

Didn't you know that Edgar Allan Poe
Sought grief counselling, took Lexapro?
No longer then by endless mourning smitten
He'd left lugubrious laments to diverse
Obsequies by Thomas Holley Chivers.
But we've not seen the poems he must have written—
Like Nathaniel Parker Willis's, say?
No, no, much wittier, Poe's *vers de société*.
Surely his *jeux d'esprit* deserve a tranche
Of the renown of Christopher Pearse Cranch—
Were he but free of personal disaster
He might well be our Minor Light Verse Master,
Poe's doppelgänger and abiding dream,
Undone, for aye, by his one remorseless theme.

A Happy Poet

Last night, when Perri and Dave came over for a drink or
Two, as we sat before the fire and reminisced,
Dave suddenly broke in to say
In that basement flat they'd had at 11th and Spruce,
The one where, first married, they had to lay
The tiles themselves, he'd found, when crouched

On hands and knees to place a square behind
The door, taped on the inside jamb, way down
So you wouldn't see it, a paper strip the size
Of the fortune in a cookie, and he read,
"A Happy Poet is a Crock of Shit"

                                  —Oh, who, who, who
Would have spelled out that crude complaint and taped it
Inside the door so no one could read?
Dave, himself a poet , thought it was
A poet who'd been Happy but, disillusioned,
His best friend had stolen his girl, so he

Could be no longer Happy, and hated himself
For having been so Happy, so full of a trust
That was betrayed—
                      But Perri thought the screed the cry
Of a former tenant whose best friend,
The Happy Poet, had stolen his girl, so now

He hated his old friend for being Happy
While he was bitter and had hid the message
As a curse, where Happy wouldn't see it,
And wouldn't know why his luck was bad, or why
The girl deserted him for her former
Boyfriend—we tossed this around

Much of the night, still wondered
Was it a Poet who had written that?
Hard to believe a real poet would say
'I'm Happy' with such a stale, dumb cliché,
When he could have better taped onto the door
The same conviction, but in metaphor—

A Happy Poet's a Goldfinch in a Tree
About to Feed a Raging Forest Fire,
A Goldfish in a bowl Who Cannot See
It's Leaking, A Happy Poet Dreams of Higher
Jackpots than the One He Just Has Won
But his next roll will be a pair of twos,

Betraying all his fond desire,
And his days of Happiness are done . . .
Is this a fable of the Poet's role?
Do true Poems come from some Happy soul?
Who needs to write, or wants to read, the story
Of one whose love-life, like his world, is hunky-dory?

No, the H.P. must endure the curse
Of an illusion, for he can write no verse
That lasts unless torn from the living leaf
Of his despair, his sorrow, or his grief.
His lines, if we remember them, will flow
From a pen dipped in the deep inkwell of woe.

Well, that's settled . . . Felt good to get it right,
And then we, rather gravely, said Goodnight.

Last Words

Leaned close, to speak through your sedated sleep,
Hoping you'd hear my words, the last you'd keep
With you wherever it is you have to go.
I told again of the Paradise we know—
You, young, laughing, hand trailing the stern
As I pull on the oars and we glide on

Toward Pond Island across the glittering bay,
Our private continent to explore. Now we
Have, on a ledge, one seal for our companion.
We'll strip, plunge in the pond warmed by the sun,
Then climb the hillock, seek our mossy place,
Two becoming one in our embrace—

But why do sky and bay darken to black,
The island disappear in silvery mist?
I must press on, there is no turning back . . .
On your floating bier you lie at rest.
I vow, I'll not abandon you, we'll go
Together wherever it is you have to go,

And steer us toward insufferably white
Shrouds of fog . . .
                    Pierced by spears of light,
My eyes, prized open, recognize a room,
A dresser, mirror, jewel case, *eau de parfum*
Ownerless now. And I, adrift, alone,
Feel words cut in my heart, as on a stone.

Bands

"As her finger swelled they cut and bent this off."
He looked at it. "Well, it will be
Small, might fit her pinky."
                                        "Why? Did they
Chop out a piece?" With a magnifying
Glass he peered inside and read,
"D.G.H. to E.Mc
                5, 1948"
"Oh, that should read E.McF., 22.5 for 22nd of May—
See, here's mine, we gave them to each other."
He said, "I've had bands like this before, I've filled
The gap by soldering a cross to join
The broken ends. It helps to know
Her finger size."
                     I said, "She won't be wearing it"

—I'll put it with her ashes in the urn
And bury it behind her weathered stone,
Maine granite from Dave Buell's quarry.
By June, Jack Jackson will have carved her name
And dates, and the inscription—
As in her slanting hand across the leaf
Of her first gift to me,
Like gold to aery thinness beat,
Knowing I knew the line it followed,
"Our two souls which therefore are one."
When hers is done he'll have the time
To letter on my matching stone,
"It's more-than-lifelong love that joins us two
With serendipity, as in a rhyme."

When he can add my final date
Our legend then will be complete . . .

"I'll have this mended in a week,"
He said, and gave me the receipt.

The Key

I take our luggage down the steps
to the courtyard, it's been a long
and arduous trip and we peer through
the wrought-iron gate, curved in whorls,
elaborate work, into the garden, roses blooming,
    sunflowers and phlox, a granite
path to the doorway of the house,
old fieldstone, weathered, roofed with slate,
where we've a lifelong lease. Let's go
in!—But the gate, the gate is locked, and I
remember, have to get the key, so
leave you—it will be just a few short minutes,
leave you sitting among our cases, scent of roses
wafting toward you through the gate. I start
for the Tower, am on a little alleyway
of shops, deserted café—a woman
at curbside table asks Are you in the Gaelic Mod
at Baddeck? No, my wife knitted this hat.
Where's Market Street? Turn left
at the corner, into courtyard, walk
through nave on old memorial stones
the students rub for images, a verger points
me down a flight of stairs, through grotto where
we took snapshots of one another
in The Cloisters, this grizzled man
in a beret, he's the one we found asleep
before his cave, who said, *M'sieu, 'Dame,
suivez moi et vous serez bien guidé,*
see mastadon and images of elk
scratched on wall in smoky passageway,
dim light, the grimy furnace-tender points
me toward a street of little shops, haven't I

been here before? Now, in Caldwell's store,
silver earrings, watches, clocks, then rows
of curving women's legs in colored stockings,
next a room of suitcases then suits, high-ceilinged
lobby with big eagle statue, up
a flight, where I'm to get the key—sign
says they want deposit, look in wallet,
don't have this country's bills,
a credit card will do? *Won't take American
Express, you need a Visa here.* I sign,
she lifts the huge key from the wall,
handle filigreed in iron, must be wrought
at forge where Amish smithy shod
that horse in Paradise, PA, key
too big, too heavy for pocket, tight in hand—
I'm coming to rejoin you, we'll be together,
open the gate and settle in, so hurry
through hall of legs and suits and watches,
earrings, courtyard, street of shops, down smoky
passage through nave, alley of cafes, all empty,
and now, at last, I see—here,
the fancy gate between us and the roses,
there's our suitcases, but where, but where,
where are you? I'm at the gate,
peer through, look in the garden, then
look up, look down the empty street, you
not here, not there—could you
have somehow got inside? I look, I call
your name, your name—no answer—call your name,
I have the key, the heavy key, I'll turn it
in the gate—but there is no keyhole,
gate is locked, no keyhole, no way to get in,

you're gone, gone, beyond the garden, empty garden
while among the luggage of our lives
I'm at this gate I cannot open,
can't get in, can't get in, can't open—
you're gone, you're gone, you're gone . . .

Night Journey

After thrusting
through thickets, a tangled
way opens in
darkness. Air's tinged

with odor of leafmould,
fishscales, salt
on seabreeze. Branches part,
I break from where basalt

on beach and dark glints
of sea stretch before.
At tide's edge, tongues
of an untended fire,

and out on black water
as through a pinhole afar
light spills, comes nearer,
torchblaze on a bier.

When it touches the shore
my lost love rises
and, holding the flame,
beckons, calling my name—

we flow through a halflight
throbbing with silence.
Applescent sifts the air
as we glide among islands.

There, thronging the shore
to welcome us, crowds

call, and gesture.
The wind stirs their shrouds.

My tall Grandpa's there
and my Dad—"You've come
too soon, too far.
You haven't done

what you have to do . . ."
"What is that?" I cry,
but a great fogbank furls
the island from my view

and what it was they reply
becomes one with the sway
of the sea, as the light pries
my eyes to the day.

Today

Today the sun rose, as it used to do
When its mission was to shine on you.
Since in unforgiving dark you're gone,
What purpose has the sun?

[2007]

Soul

How strange it is that 'soul'
Is obsolescent now,
Like 'abode,' or, maybe, 'domicile'—

Everybody knows
What you mean by it,
But who has, or lives in, one?

As though soul's the house then,
Not a tenant
Who outlives the lease

Or maybe soul is neither
A perpetual sensorium
Nor its own dwelling-place,

But like the magnitude of light
By which a heavenly body
Cleaves the emptiness of night

It is a resident
Property
Of the body, living

While it lives,
A conveyance from afar
Of pure intensity

That is a consummation
Of itself, consuming
What it gives.

Afterlife

(i.m. Elizabeth McFarland)

It must be easier if one believes
The soul's immortal, and survives someplace,
Say in Heaven, where it keeps its face
And to such singularity each cleaves,

Or, as in childhood, when I used to think
That souls were points of light in the Milky Way,
Casting their sight on us, as though to say
Between two worlds there's but a casual link,

And whenever someone died a brand new star
Would suddenly appear in the distant sky;
There'd be no dissolution, then, to die,
Existing ever, a grain of light, afar—

But you and I, free of such superstition,
Lived and loved each other with each breath,
And now I know the love that transcends death,
Keeping you in memory's inner vision,

But where is personhood when one is gone?
As body is reclaimed by earth, or flame,
Does Death's sharp saber-tooth exempt a name
So those who loved you feel you linger on?

You, when young, dreamed you'd become a tree,
Where words gathered among your blossoming
Branches, bickered, birdlike. You made them sing,
As now, in verse alive with *bel esprit*—

Don't fade into your photos . . . for you lift
My spirits, those of friends, and of all who feel
The joy, the wit, the passion your lines reveal,
So like your love, an imperishable gift.

Acknowledgments

Some of these poems are slightly altered from their first appearances in the following publications:

American Arts Quarterly: "Eve Reclining"
Boulevard: "A Happy Poet"
Early American Literature: "Freneau"
First Things: "Icons"
Gettysburg Review: "The Hill"
Hudson Review: "Afterlife," "Bands," "Spring," and "Then"
Mad Poets Review: "Other Bodies"
The New Criterion: "At 89," "A Democratic Vista," and "Darts, 1965"
New Ohio Review: "Awareness" and "Night Journey"
On Earth: "A Wilding"
per contra: "A Poe Taster" and "A Riddle"
Poetry: "Today"
Sewanee Review: "Interplanetary Converse," "Last Words," "Raven," and "Soul"
Vanderbilt Review: "The Day"

These were first published in earlier books of mine:

"For Whom I Make This Song" (untitled), in *A Little Geste and Other Poems* (1960)
"At the Winter Solstice," in *The City of Satisfactions* (1963)
"In Memory of Lewis Corey," in *Broken Laws* (1970)

and

"Life-Lines," in *Richard Eberhart: A Celebration,* edited by Sidney Lea et al. (1980)
"A Democratic Vista," in *Best American Poetry 2009,* edited by David Wagoner (2009)

Notes

"Interplanetary Converse"

After receiving the Nobel Prize for medicine, Baruch Blumberg became head of the Astrobiology Institute. His obituary in the *New York Times* said that he "and his team were asked . . . How does life begin and evolve? Does life exist elsewhere in the universe? And what is life's future on Earth and beyond . . . He said he would be 'very surprised, if we found something in space, that it would look like E.T. If we found something more like a virus or a bacteria, that would be astounding enough.'"

"In Memory of Lewis Corey"

Born Luigi Fraina (Salerno, 1898), he was brought to New York at six, and left school when his father died. A brilliant boy, he quickly matured into radical politics and love of the arts. He soon led the left, tilting it toward Communism, and helped found the American Communist Party. By 1920, he was a delegate to the Comintern in Moscow.

"Madison Square Garden": Fraina led a mass rally denouncing U.S. and British invasion of Archangel to overturn the Russian Revolution.

"Moscow Trials": False confessions, often under torture, in show trials of all the Old Bolsheviks, on Stalin's orders executed or exiled to Siberia, 1936–1938.

In Moscow Fraina was accused of being a U.S. spy. Disillusioned by the conspiratorial suspicions, rigidity, and narrow ideology of Communism, he rejected the movement, took the name Lewis Corey as a new identity, and became an independent Marxian critic. The Red press excoriated him, an apostate.

In 1934 his much-praised book, *The Decline of American Capitalism,* proposed a reformist, moderate middle class to heal the economic injustices of the Great Depression. Though he never finished high school, he was made a professor of economics at Antioch College. In 1944–1946, I was in the Army Air Force—stationed at nearby Wright Field—and when commissioned, lived off-base in Yellow Springs, Ohio, where I met Corey's daughter Olga and soon Corey himself.

By the 1950s, Senator Joseph McCarthy's accusations of Communism had poisoned American public life. The FBI invited testimony from a "hireling liar," later indicted for perjury, who named Corey a Communist spy. Fired from his job with a union, Corey was ordered deported. This persecution brought on the stroke that killed him in 1953.

An anomaly in American politics, he was a European-style intellectual who was also deeply interested in poetry, dance, and music. At his death he was writing on the poetry of Heinrich Heine.

A fuller account of all this appears on pp. 90–97 of my wartime memoir, *Zone of the Interior* (2000).

"Reading the News, 1968"

Race riots erupted in major cities after the assassination of Martin Luther King on April 4. In Washington, D.C., there was violence and looting, and fires burned for five days.

"History, 1989"

On June 5, the army of the People's Republic of China crushed the prodemocracy demonstration of hundreds of students in Tiananmen Square. A replica of the Statue of Liberty was their inspiration. The scene described was televised and shown frequently for weeks.

"The Hill"

Glu'uskap, in Penobscot mythology, was the spiritual being who brought good into the world and possessed the powers described.

"Darts, 1965"

The centenary year of W. B. Yeats. I lectured that summer at the Yeats School in Sligo.

"Afterlife"

The penultimate stanza alludes to, and quotes, "Myself" by Elizabeth McFarland:

> I have stood so long in this place
> I have lost account of my face.
> I have stared so long at this tree
> I am grown blossomy.
> In my branches, words
> Bicker like birds.

This was among her poems that won the Freshman Writing Contest at Florida State College for Women in 1941, when she was eighteen. It is the first poem in her book, *Over the Summer Water* (Orchises Press, 2008).

About the Author

Daniel Hoffman served as Poet Laureate in 1973–74, when the appointment was called Consultant in Poetry of The Library of Congress. His first book, *An Armada of Thirty Whales,* was W. H. Auden's choice for the Yale Series of Younger Poets Award in 1954. Among his dozen subsequent volumes are *Brotherly Love,* a finalist in 1981 for both the National Book Award and the National Book Critics Circle Award; *Beyond Silence: Selected Shorter Poems 1948–2003;* and *The Whole Nine Yards: Longer Poems.* Best known of his critical studies are *The Poetry of Stephen Crane, Faulkner's Country Matters,* and another National Book Award finalist, *Poe Poe Poe Poe Poe Poe Poe.* His late wife was the poet and editor Elizabeth McFarland, whose posthumous book of poems, *Over the Summer Water,* he compiled in 2008. Hoffman is retired from the University at Pennsylvania as the Felix E. Schelling Professor Emeritus of English, and lives in Pennsylvania and on Cape Rosier in Maine.

www.ingramcontent.com/pod-product-compliance
Lightning Source LLC
Chambersburg PA
CBHW030122170426
43198CB00009B/711